THE POWER OF THE GRACE OF GOD

"But by the grace of God I am what I am: and his grace which was bestowed upon me was not in vain;..."

1Cor15:10

By
Franklin N. Abazie

The Power of the Grace of God

COPYRIGHT 2018 BY Franklin N Abazie
ISBN: 978-1-945-133-58-9
All right reserved. This book or any portion thereof may not be reproduced or used in any manner whatsoever without the express written permission of the publisher, except for the use of brief quotations in a book review. All Bible quotes are from King James Version and others as noted.

Published by: F N ABAZIE PUBLISHING HOUSE---
a.k.a,
Empowerment Bookstore:

That I may publish with the voice of thanksgiving and tell of all thy wondrous works. **Psalms26:7**

To order additional copies, wholesales or booking: Call the Church office (973-372-7518)
or Empowerment Bookstore Hotline 973-393-8518
Worship address:
343 Sanford Avenue Newark New Jersey 07106
Administrative Head Office address:
33 Schley Street Newark New Jersey 07112
Email:pastorfranknto@yahoo.com
Website www.fnabaziehealingministries.org
Publishing House: www.fnabaziepublishinghouse.org

This book is a production of F N Abazie
Publishing House.

A publication Arms of Miracle of God Ministries 2018
First Edition

CONTENTS

THE MANDATE OF THE COMMISSION............iv

ARMS OF THE COMMISSION............................v

INTRODUCTION...viii

CHAPTER 1

1. What is the Grace of God?................................22

CHAPTER 2

2. How to Live by the Grace of God......................29

CHAPTER 3

3. Prayer of Salvation...83

CHAPTER 4

4. About the Author..94

THE MANDATE OF THE COMMISSION

"THE MOMENT IS DUE TO IMPACT YOUR WORLD THROUGH THE REVIVAL OF THE HEALING & MIRACLE MINISTRY OF JESUS CHRIST OF NAZARETH.

I AM SENDING YOU TO RESTORE HEALTH UNTO THEE AND I WILL HEAL THEE OF THY WOUNDS, SAID THE LORD OF HOST."

ARMS OF THE COMMISSION

1) F N Abazie Ministries-Miracle of God Ministries (Miracle Chapel Intl)

2) F N Abazie TV Ministries: Global Television Ministry Outreach.

3) F N Abazie Radio Ministries: Radio Broadcasting Outreach.

4) F N Abazie Publishing House: Book Publication.

5) F N Abazie Bible School: also called Word of Healing Bible School (W.O.H.B.S)

6) F N Abazie Evangelistic Ass: Miracle of God Ministries: Global Crusade

7) Empowerment Bookstore: Book distribution.

8) F N Abazie Helping Hands: Meeting the help of the needy world wide

9) F N Abazie Disaster Recovery Mission: Global Disaster Recovery.

10) F N Abazie Prison Ministry: Prison Ministry for all convicts "Second chance"

Some of our ministry arms are waiting the appointed time to commence

FAVOR CONFESSION

Father thank you for making me righteous and accepted through the blood of Jesus Christ. Because of that, I am blessed and highly favored by God. I am the subject of your affection. Your favor surrounds me as a shield, and the first thing that people see around me is your favored shield.

Thank you that I have favor with you and man today. All day long people go out of their way to bless me and help me. I have favor with everyone that I deal with today. Doors that were once closed are now opened for me. I receive preferential treatment, and I have special privileges, I am Gods favored child.

No good thing will he withhold from me. Because of Gods favor my enemies cannot triumph over my life. I have supernatural increase and promotion. I declare restoration to everything that the devil has stolen from my life. I have honor in the midst of my adversaries and an increase in assets, especially in real estate and expansion of territories.

Because I am highly favored by God, I experience great victories, supernatural turnarounds, and miraculous breakthrough in the midst of great impossibilities. I receive recognition, prominence, and honor. Petitions are granted to me even by ungodly authorities. Policies, rules, regulations, and laws are changed and reverse on my behalf.

I win battles that I don't even have to fight, because God fights them for me. This is the day, the set time and the designated moment for me to experience the free favor of God, that profusely and lavishly abound on my behalf in Jesus name. Amen.

INTRODUCTION

"...and he shall bring forth the headstone thereof with shoutings, crying, Grace, grace unto it." **Zecharia4:7**

The Grace of God simply means divine help from God. The Grace of God is what makes great in the kingdom of God. Outside this kingdom people talk about talent, wisdom, intelligent. In the Kingdom of God, grace is what makes great.

"But by the grace of God I am what I am: and his grace which was bestowed upon me was not in vain; but I laboured more abundantly than they all: yet not I, but the grace of God which was with me." **1cor15:10.**

The Grace of God is all it takes for an exciting life in the kingdom of God. Apostle Paul confessed *"But by the grace of God I am what I am: and his grace which was bestowed upon me was not in vain..."*

The teaching in this book is to boast our faith in God. The truth is we need God's divine grace and help to succeed in this great times we live in.

It is written *"Then he answered and spake unto me, saying, This is the word of the Lord unto Zerubbabel, saying, Not by might, nor by power, but by my spirit, saith the Lord of hosts."* **Zecharia4:6**

The grace of God is all it takes to succeed in the kingdom of God hear this "And with great power the apostles gave witness to the resurrection of the Lord Jesus. And great grace was upon them all." Acts 4:33.

"... but grow in the grace and knowledge of our Lord and Savior Jesus Christ." **(2 Peter 3:18)**

"You therefore, my son, be strong in the grace that is in Christ Jesus." **(2 Timothy 2:1).**

I pray this small book release the divine virtue of God hidden inside His grace. Come with me as the Holy Spirit unfold the untold stories of the grace of God.

Happy reading.

HIS DESTINY WAS THE CROSS….

HIS PURPOSE WAS LOVE…..

HIS REASON WAS YOU….

"After you have suffered for a little while, the God of all grace, who called you to His eternal glory in Christ, will Himself perfect, confirm, strengthen and establish you." **1 Peter 5:10**

"Through Silvanus, our faithful brother (for so I regard him), I have written to you briefly, exhorting and testifying that this is the true grace of God Stand firm in it." **1 Peter 5:12**

"As each one has received a special gift, employ it in serving one another as good stewards of the manifold grace of God." **1 Peter 4:10**

"But I do not consider my life of any account as dear to myself, so that I may finish my course and the ministry which I received from the Lord Jesus, to testify solemnly of the gospel of the grace of God." **Acts 20:24**

"Then when he arrived and witnessed the grace of God, he rejoiced and began to encourage them all with resolute heart to remain true to the Lord;" **Acts 11:23**

"Which has come to you, just as in all the world also it is constantly bearing fruit and increasing, even as it has been doing in you also since the day you heard of it and understood the grace of God in truth;" **Colossians 1:6**

"But we do see Him who was made for a little while lower than the angels, namely, Jesus, because of the suffering of death crowned with glory and honor, so that by the grace of God He might taste death for everyone." **Hebrews 2:9**

"And now I commend you to God and to the word of His grace, which is able to build you up and to give you the inheritance among all those who are sanctified." **Acts 20:32**

"But the free gift is not like the transgression. For if by the transgression of the one the many died, much more did the grace of God and the gift by the grace of the one Man, Jesus Christ, abound to the many." **Romans 5:15**

"For if by the transgression of the one, death reigned through the one, much more those who receive the abundance of grace and of the gift of righteousness will reign in life through the One, Jesus Christ." **Romans 5:17**

"And when he wanted to go across to Achaia, the brethren encouraged him and wrote to the disciples to welcome him; and when he had arrived, he greatly helped those who had believed through grace." **Acts 18:27**

"But when God, who had set me apart even from my mother's womb and called me through His grace, was pleased." **Galatians 1:15**

"Or do you think lightly of the riches of His kindness and tolerance and patience, not knowing that the kindness of God leads you to repentance?" **Romans 2:4**

"Behold then the kindness and severity of God; to those who fell, severity, but to you, God's kindness, if you continue in His kindness; otherwise you also will be cut off." **Romans 11:22**

"Behold then the kindness and severity of God; to those who fell, severity, but to you, God's kindness, if you continue in His kindness; otherwise you also will be cut off." **Romans 11:22**

"So that in the ages to come He might show the surpassing riches of His grace in kindness toward us in Christ Jesus." **Ephesians 2:7**

"How much severer punishment do you think he will deserve who has trampled under foot the Son of God, and has regarded as unclean the blood of the covenant by which he was sanctified, and has insulted the Spirit of grace?" **Hebrews 10:29**

"With the kind You show Yourself kind, With the blameless You show Yourself blameless;" **2 Samuel 22:26**

"With the kind You show Yourself kind; With the blameless You show Yourself blameless;" **Psalm 18:25**

"You have been severed from Christ, you who are seeking to be justified by law; you have fallen from grace." **Galatians 5:4**

All Sufficiency in All Things
(2 Corinthians 9:8)

All sufficiency in all things means that we lack nothing in any area of life. I don't know about you but I am ready for that. It does not mean that we will never be tested but once we have passed the test and remain faithful, we will have all sufficiency. Many have been going through a time of testing for some time now. During this time of financial crisis, God wants to bring you out into a place of sufficiency. He will do so when things are looking bad everywhere else so that both you and the world will know it is God.

We Must Abound to Every Good Work
(2 Corinthians 9:8)

God doesn't bless us for blessing sake alone. He does so for a purpose. He blesses us in order that we might be a blessing **(Genesis 12:2)**. When He gives you sufficiency in all things He expects you to be faithful with what He has given you.

In other words, when you see a need He expects you to take from your abundance and meet that need. Take from the blessings He has bestowed upon you and do good with it and that in abundance.

Give Thanks to God
(2 Corinthians 9:11-13)

When we give to meet the needs of others (people and ministries) it produces thanksgiving and praise to God. Paul is literally saying that as we give liberally it increases the worship of God. People begin praising God (increase their praise and its intensity) because of the grace you have shown through your giving.

Increasing Prayer on Our Behalf
(2 Corinthians 9:14)

As you give liberally, you are purchasing prayer on your behalf. As you bless and meet the needs of others through your giving, reason dictates they will pray for you more and with greater intensity.

"They will pray for you with deep affection because of the overflowing grace God has given to you" **(2 Corinthians 9:14).**

Let's believe that God will begin to bestow upon His people an abundance of financial grace, in spite of what may be going on in the world around us.

Stages of salvation

Justification is when the soul is set free from the penalty of sin. **1 John 1:9** – *"If we confess our sins, he is faithful and just and will forgive us our sins and purify us from all unrighteousness."*

Sanctification is when the soul is set free from the power of sin. **John 17:17** – *"For this is the will of God, even your sanctification."*

Glorification is when the soul is set free from the possibility of sin.

1 John 1:3 – *"Dear friends, now we are children of God, and what we will be has not yet been made known. But we know that when he appears, we shall be like him."*

We enter the door of sanctification the moment we consecrate our lives to Christ and submit ourselves to the process of becoming more like Him. Justification and sanctification are pre-requisites for glorification when salvation is finally complete. Glorification occurs after the death of the body when the soul is transported beyond the reach of temptation and sin.

Salvation is not complete until we have been glorified. Philippians 1:6 says, *"He who has started a good work in you will carry it on to completion."* But, God seems to have tempered his own sovereignty by gifting man with free will.

Christians are certainly eternally secure, but this security is conditional. It could be disrupted by the sovereignty of God or the free will God has given man.

Can a man lose his salvation? I don't think so. Romans 8:38 says, *"For I am convinced that nothing can ever separate us from God's love."*

Paul goes on to list all of the things that are incapable of separating us from God's love. But, Paul does not include ourselves in that list. Can a man choose to become an apostate? The Bible seems to indicate that a man can choose to walk away from God.

There are at least 80 passages of in the New Testament that teach that the process of salvation can be interrupted, delayed or stopped altogether. Jude 21 says, *"keep yourselves in God's love"* and Jude 24 says, *"He is able to keep you."* This seems to indicate a conditional relationship. He will keep us if we will determine to be kept.

Jesus declared himself to be the true vine. Dead branches are cut away and destroyed while fruitful branches are pruned so they will produce even more fruit **(John 15:4).**

Christ warns against the prevalent teaching of cheap grace. Hebrews 10:26-27 says, *"If we deliberately keep on sinning after we have received the knowledge of the truth, no sacrifice for sins is left, but only a fearful expectation of judgment and of raging fire that will consume the enemies of God."*

1 Peter 2:20 says, *"It would have been better for them not to have known the way of righteousness, than to have known it and then to turn their backs on the sacred command that was passed on to them."*

Peter is saying that people who enter the way and then departed from it are worse off. This is contradictory for those who argue that we might continue to live a sinful lifestyle and still be rewarded with eternal life. If they received eternal life how are they worse off?

I question the idea that we cannot walk away from God because it seems to make God inconsistent. Either he has gifted us with free will or he has not.

But I argue that it is very unlikely that a man would choose to walk away from God if he were truly, genuinely saved. Maybe a more accurate statement would be not so much, *"once saved always saved"* but *"if saved always saved."*

CHAPTER 1
What is the Grace of God?

The Grace of God; if I could put it this way, means! God-- *in the race of the life of man.* The grace of God literally means *"God's exemption for us from divine judgment."*

It is written *"And of his fulness have all we received, and grace for grace. For the law was given by Moses, but grace and truth came by Jesus Christ."* **John1:16-17**

If God was to take account of all we do wrong daily who can stand before Him?" We are told *"Grace and peace be multiplied unto you through the knowledge of God, and of Jesus our Lord."* **2Peter1:2**

The word of God says, *"If thou, Lord, shouldest mark iniquities, O Lord, who shall stand? But there is forgiveness with thee, that thou mayest be feared."* **Psalms130:3-4**

Although, the *Grace of God* has been defined in so many different ways. Whenever we think of God's grace we remember of the gift of Jesus for the redemption of sin-- *"Salvation."* I love to say that Grace simply means, *"God, giving us what we don't deserve."* We deserved the punishment of sin and death, but Jesus died for us all on the cross.

The word of God says, *"If thou, Lord, shouldest mark iniquities, O Lord, who shall stand? But there is forgiveness with thee, that thou mayest be feared."* **Psalms 130:3-4**
So knowing about God's grace causes us to seek to know just how to show grace to others.

So knowing about God's grace causes us to seek to know just how to show grace to others.

Although no one can offer salvation to another person, we can be kind and gracious to them. Showing grace to others is a matter of dealing kindly with them, even if they don't deserve it.

Chapter 1 - What is the Grace of God?

Showing Grace With Words

When speaking with people you should use words that are kind and gentle. Obviously, there are times we need to correct other people, but it never has to be done in a resentful or hateful manner. We can be gentle with our word.

It is written, *"Let no corrupt communication proceed out of your mouth, but that which is good to the use of edifying, that it may minister grace unto the hearers."* **Ephesians4:29**

How To Show Grace

Can you help someone in some small way?

Look for the Needs of Others

Can you help someone in some small way? Holding a door for someone whose arms are full can be a small action that helps in a great way.

If you will seek out little actions you can do for others it will help you become a more graceful person. Don't just look for opportunities to fulfill monumental needs. Our ability to change other people's lives with large financial donations or heroic actions are seldom within our grasp, but we can affect people every day with simple kindnesses.

Respond With Grace

Have you been criticized by someone? Even unjustly? You don't have to let others walk over you, but you can respond in a gracious way. Accept what they have to say and thank them for their input.

The news they bring you may upset you and hurt you deeply. The way you respond can help the healing process to begin immediately. A quick response with anger will leave you seething. But the sooner you can respond with a smile and a calm spirit the sooner you will be able to see the truth in their words and make the changes that need to be made.

Chapter 1 - What is the Grace of God?

Graceful Presence

Take opportunities to be with someone in a time of grief. They don't need you to deliver some special speech or do anything grand for them and the family. Your presence may be all that is needed to show you love them.

Funerals and hospital stays are times when you can make a quick visit that will leave an impact in someone's life. You don't have to spend hours with them, but they do want to know you care and that you are thinking of them. Even if it is just a brief visit, stopping by to say hello can mean the world to them in their time of physical or emotional pain.

Forgive With Grace

When someone asks forgiveness, accept their apology graciously. They have come to you humbly asking for your pardon. That is not a time to tell them why they should have done so much sooner. Nor is it an appropriate time to correct them and tell them how they could have handled the situation better.

If you are in a teaching or authoritative position over the person and you need to give them advice that will help them in the future, separate your advice from your forgiveness. Allow them to see you have accepted their apology and then later share with them the correction and direction they need.

Learn to say *"I'm Sorry."*

When you make a mistake, swallow your pride and ask for forgiveness. Maybe they wronged you in some way but you responded inappropriately.

You can ask them to forgive you for your response. Remember grace is giving to the other person what they don't deserve. Even if, in your opinion, they don't deserve an apology, you can ask their forgiveness for your wrong response.

Chapter 1 - What is the Grace of God?

Keep Short Accounts

When you need to apologize, do it quickly. Don't keep a running total of how many times they have done wrong towards you. Forgive, even if they don't ask for it. Grace can go a long way to repairing a relationship if you will respond in a loving way, even when they don't.

Clean Up Your Language

Beyond using gentle words with those around you, be careful how you express yourself. Do you have some words in your vocabulary that shouldn't be there? There may be some words you say that aren't really "bad" words, but the way you say them express the same feelings as your co-worker's curse words. Be careful with substitute curse words. Even if you aren't saying the same thing, you mean exactly the same emotions as others who use the real words.

Say Thank You To Show Grace To Others

Take time to say *"thank you."* It doesn't cost anything, but it can show other people gratitude and grace. Write a simple card expressing your appreciation for a kind act on your behalf. You can make a difference by putting a *"thank you"* on your lips and a card in someone's hand.

Take Interest in Others

I do not know much about you but Often it makes me feel good when people take interest in my affairs. It is a good thing to take interest in another people. grief with those that are grieving, mourn with those that are mourning. laugh with those that are laughing.

"Let your speech be always with grace, seasoned with salt, that ye may know how ye ought to answer every man." **Colossians 4:6**

CHAPTER 2
How to Live by the Grace of God

Without any revelation from God, we all have been living by *the grace of God* for a very long time now. Think about it! If God was to judge all our wrong actions today, none of us will escape it. *But I thank God for His mercy and grace upon our lives. To live by the grace of God is to live in peace with all men. To live by the grace of God is to take interest in the affairs of others. To laugh with those that are laughing and to mourn with those that are mourning in life.*

According to the Law of Reciprocal Action, everything, good or bad, returns back to man. Nothing can be forgiven, but all must be paid until the last penny. As it says in the Bible, a good tree will produce good fruit and a bad tree will produce bad fruit, no matter we like it or not, whether we believe it or not.

Let's see how such *"forgiveness of sins"* looks like in practice. Man is thinking about what he's done a couple of minutes and then he "regrets" his deeds. And thereby he considers the whole thing terminated.

He does not try to make any effort to change his inner self. Why would he do it? After all, he was told to only regret and eventually to say a few prayers as a sign of repentance – and the Grace of God should put everything back in order. Such a pity is only a deceptive appeasement of conscience and has no real effect. Confessionals are still full of sinners and man does the same unpleasant things over and over again, often during his whole life.

The usual act of regretting sins does not work primarily because just then man deals with his past, although, recent acts; so basically he is thinking about how he was, not how he is. The bad personality traits that led him to the wrong doing and which must be removed, are still present in him, not in the past.

The past is only a memory of our mind, not a tangible reality, in which we can feel and change anything. Therefore, man is almost always able to continue acting the same wrong way no matter he believes in "God's Grace" and confesses.

Chapter 2 - How to Live by the Grace of God

As long as he is not seeking the way to get rid of his personality flaws and instead of doing so, he is dealing with a "dead" past, he cannot succeed. Thinking about past acts is only good for better self-knowledge, so that we know how we are and what we need to change inside ourselves in the present. Excessive thinking and dwelling on the past would distract us from life in the present, keep us depressed from seeing who we once were and thus darken us even more.

The real change must take place within us, not within our thoughts. Regretful thoughts are too shallow to touch the spirit and change something on human nature. If man wants to change, he has to feel the existing disharmony inside him in his heart. It is not enough to know that he acted improperly – he must imminently feel this improperness within himself.

Feel so truly and deeply that he will never be able to do anything like that again, because he will feel disgust towards such deeds from the depth of his soul.

Knowing the truth about what wrongful acting causes must be simply stronger than the sweet desire to sin. Only then is it possible to receive the gift of God's Grace.

Even if the promised forgiveness really worked, there would be still one more serious fact, which is, while relying on "all forgiving Grace of God", often forgotten – man did not make the due amends for the damage he had caused by his misconduct. And that is the moment when real God's Grace can be applied.

In order to understand correctly in what the Grace of God consists of, it is necessary to be aware of the existing Divine laws, which determine the way how the forces in the Creation interact. According to one of these laws, only the forces of the same kind can affect each other.

Chapter 2 - How to Live by the Grace of God

You are certainly familiar with the manifestation of this law in the material world: you cannot drill a hole into the water; you cannot bend the air with hammer thumps, you cannot catch the radio waves with a butterfly net; etc., because these elements have different nature.

Now, let's take a look at how this law applies to the human deeds:\r\nImagine two people who, long ago, intentionally harmed someone's health. Let's suppose that one of them realized the wrongness of his actions and changed himself; the other one, however, did not, and has even defined his actions as the law of the strongest, having considered them right.

Regardless how he justified his own actions, the harm he has caused will return back to him. In addition to pain, mockery and limited life opportunities of the harmed person, there are also the worsened life conditions of harmed person's family which must be added to the consequences of the harm.

For example, due to the lack of funds, his children might be deprived from the opportunity of living their childhood fully, of having the desired education, which may bring another negative consequences charged to the account of the man who has caused the harm in the first place. And we cannot even imagine how many similar negative consequences are related to wrong acts.

The harvest of human deeds is usually much greater than the seeds we sowed; in a similar way to the mustard seeds that give rise to several meters tall plants whose seeds grow into another and another plants.\r\nHow will the reverse effect of those deeds look inside such different people?

The one who saw his act as wrong and changed himself to a better person is now radiating light and bright vibrations, to which heavy and dark vibrations, returning due to his previous deeds, cannot lean. The bad effects will hit him only with reduced force, proportionally to how much of the dark vibrations he removed from his personality.

Chapter 2 - How to Live by the Grace of God

In case that no darkness is found inside him, the bad effects will just miss him.

Unlike him, the man who did not change himself will be hit with full force by the returning effects of his erstwhile deed, because these returning dark vibrations will find inside him full support for their activities. The effect will be huge and the man will probably end up in a wheelchair. Alas, if he has not managed to realize what his behavior had caused and continued to act ruthlessly! He must experience himself the harm he caused to others.

The Law of Uniformity protects people from unnecessary suffering by allowing encounters only between forces of the same kind. Why should the man who has already changed himself suffer for his past acts? It would not bring him any benefit.

It would be only a sign of imperfection, which is excluded from the perfect Divine laws.

Suffering is necessary only for obdurate people who are unable to recognize wrongness of their actions other than by experiencing the evil they caused for themselves.

If man is conceited, calculating, selfish, malicious, or has other dark traits within himself, his spiritual body will radiate the darkness as well. It will consist of heavy and dense vibrations and anything really good won't be able to reach him. Conversely, man who is generous, friendly, noble-minded, well-meaning... will radiate gentle and light vibrations of bright vivid colors. He will be open to only equally bright and beautiful forces and anything dark will not be able to hurt him seriously.

If such different people meet together, they will not find common ground easily. Therefore, everyone seeks intuitively his kind of people in accordance with the Law of Uniformity.

Chapter 2 - How to Live by the Grace of God

God's Grace is never given to those who admitted their guilt, regretted their acts and wanted to change themselves, but it is given only to those who actually changed themselves. God's Grace "recognizes" such man according to how he radiates.

It works in perfect Divine laws according to how intense is man's light or darkness, not according to what he thinks of himself. Thinking about wrongdoing does not make spirit bright and thus it does not prevent the effect of returning dark harvest.

Only there, where the spirit is not surrounded by dark radiation, but where its robe is cleaned, returning effects of past bad acts cannot find any support and "forgiveness of sins" occurs.

This is the way the Grace of God works in our lives. Even the greatest sinner can step up to the Light without having to worry about reverse effects of his past deeds crushing him down even if these effects were extremely huge.

The Grace of God consists only in this – not in a go-as-you-please forgiveness of sins for which God's Grace is incorrectly considered.

In relation to the laws, in which the Grace of God applies, it remains to be said that whereas on one hand these laws help people to overcome the consequences of their bad deeds (so called "karma"), on the other hand they also work vice versa. If man falls spiritually and his astral bodies become dark and heavy, he thus stops returning effects of his erstwhile good deeds.

Good effects will not be able to hold on to dark vibrations just as effects of his bad deeds would not be able to hit him when he changed for the better and radiated brightly.

The Law of Uniformity and the Law of Reciprocal Action lead us back to the life in the present, and the Grace of God is given to us as a huge help on our way to the Light. It does not matter what was in the past, but only how we behave now matters.

Chapter 2 - How to Live by the Grace of God

Who we are and how we radiate can not be pretended or obtained otherwise than by honest work on ourselves. Knowledge that our past faults, even the worst ones, do not stand between us, and the Light opens the way to the Light for everyone who is willing to find out what they are doing wrong and to do their best to change themselves. The Grace of God will assist them.

CONDITION TO RECEIVE THE HOLY SPIRIT

REPENTANCE

Repent, and be baptized every one of you in the name of Jesus Christ for the remission of sins, and ye shall receive the gift of the Holy Ghost.

BE BAPTIZE

".... be baptized every one of you in the name of Jesus Christ for the remission of sins, and ye shall receive the gift of the Holy Ghost." **Acts2:38**

CONFESS OF YOUR SIN

"If we confess our sins, he is faithful and just to forgive us our sins, and to cleanse us from all unrighteousness." **1John1:9**

ACKNOWLEDGMENT

"Acknowledge that you are a sinner and that Jesus Christ died for your sins." **Rom3:23.**

Chapter 2 - How to Live by the Grace of God

BORN AGAIN

"Jesus answered and said unto him, Verily, verily, I say unto thee, Except a man be born again, he cannot see the kingdom of God." **John3:3**

CONDITIONS FOR THE ACQUINTANCE OF THE HOLY SPIRIT

WALKING IN THE SPIRIT

"This I say then, Walk in the Spirit, and ye shall not fulfil the lust of the flesh."- **gal5:17**

FAITH

"We having the same spirit of faith, according as it is written, I believed, and therefore have I spoken; we also believe, and therefore speak." **2cor4:13**

WALK IN AGREEMENT

"Can two walk together, except they both agreed?" **Amos3:3**

WALK IN LOVE

"And we have known and believed the love that God hath to us. God is love; and he that dwelleth in love dwelleth in God, and God in him." **1John4:16.**

WALK IN TRUTH

"If the Son therefore shall make you free, ye shall be free indeed." **John8:32**

In Summary

The word translated *"grace"* in the New Testament comes from the Greek word charis, which means *"favor, blessing, or kindness."* We can all extend grace to others; but when the word grace is used in connection with God, it interprets a greater meaning. Grace is God choosing to bless us rather than curse us as we deserve.

It is written, *"And of his fulness have all we received, and grace for grace. For the law was given by Moses, but grace and truth came by Jesus Christ."* **John1:16-17.**

Chapter 2 - How to Live by the Grace of God

We must walk stand and live by His grace.

"But when it pleased God, who separated me from my mother's womb, and called me by his grace," **Gal1:15**

PRAYER POINTS THAT WORKS

I cancel my name and that of my family from the death register, with the fire of God, in the name of Jesus.

Every weapon of destruction fashioned against me and my family, be destroyed by the fire of God, in the name of Jesus.

Power of God, fight for me in every area of my life, in Jesus' name.

Every hindrance to my breakthrough, be melted by the fire of God, in the name of Jesus.

Every evil power against me, be scattered by the thunder fire of God, in the name of Jesus.

Father Lord, destroy every evil man/woman in the name of Jesus.

Every failures of the past, be converted to success, in Jesus' name.

Chapter 2 - How to Live by the Grace of God

Father Lord, let the former rain, the latter rain and Your blessing pour down on me now.

Father Lord, let all the failure turn into success for me, in the name of Jesus.

I receive power from on high and I paralyze all the powers of darkness that are diverting my blessings, in the name of Jesus.

Beginning from this day, I employ the services of the angels of God to open unto me every door of opportunity and breakthroughs, in the name of Jesus.

I will not go around in circles again, I will make progress, in the name of Jesus.

I shall not build for another to inhabit and I shall not plant for another to eat, in the name of Jesus.

I paralyse the powers of the emptier concerning my handiwork, in the name of Jesus.

O Lord, let every locust, caterpillar and palmer-worm assigned to eat the fruit of my labour be roasted by the fire of God.

The enemy shall not spoil my testimony in this programme, in the name of Jesus.

By the blood of Jesus, I reject every backward journey, in the name of Jesus.

By the blood of Jesus, I paralyze every strongman attached to any area of my life, in the name of Jesus.

I pray, Let every agent of shame fashioned to work against my life be paralyzed, in the name of Jesus.

I paralyse the activities of household wickedness over my life, in the name of Jesus.

I quench every strange fire emanating from evil tongues against me, in the name of Jesus.

Chapter 2 - How to Live by the Grace of God

Father Lord, give me power for maximum achievement.

Heavenly father, give me comforting authority to achieve my goal.

Blood of Jesus Christ, defend and fortify me with Your power.

I paralyse every spirit of disobedience in my life, in Jesus' name.

I refuse to disobey the voice of God, in the name of Jesus.

Every root of rebellion in my life, be uprooted, in Jesus' name.

By the blood of Jesus, I destroy every witchcraft spirit in my life, in the name of Jesus.

Contradicting forces promoting hindrance in my life, die, in Jesus' name.

Every inspiration of witchcraft in my family, be destroyed, in the name of Jesus.

Blood of Jesus, blot out every evil mark of witchcraft in my life, in the name of Jesus.

Every garment put upon me by witchcraft, be torn to pieces, in the name of Jesus.

Angels of God, begin to pursue my household enemies, let their ways be dark and slippery, in the name of Jesus.

Lord, confuse them and turn them against themselves.

By the blood of Jesus, I break every evil unconscious agreement with household enemies concerning my miracles, in the name of Jesus.

Household witchcraft, fall down and die, in the name of Jesus.

Father Lord, drag all the household wickedness to the Dead Sea and bury them there.

Chapter 2 - How to Live by the Grace of God

Father Lord, I reject to follow the evil pattern of remote control my household enemies.

My life, jump out from the cage of household wickedness, in the name of Jesus.

I command all my blessings and potentials buried by wicked household enemies to be exhumed, in the name of Jesus.

I will see the goodness of the Lord in the land of the living, in the name of Jesus.

Everything done against me to spoil my joy, receive destruction, in the name of Jesus.

Father Lord, as Abraham received favour in Your eyes, let me receive Your favour, so that I can excel in every area of my life.

Lord Jesus, help my shortcoming and infirmities in the name of Jesus.

It does not matter, whether I deserve it or not, I receive immeasurable favour from the Lord, in the name of Jesus.

By the blood of Jesus I receive every blessing God has apportioned to me in the name of Jesus.

My blessing will not be transferred to my neighbor in the name of Jesus.

Father Lord, disgrace every power that is tormenting my breakthrough in the name of Jesus.

Every step I take shall lead to outstanding success, in Jesus' name.

I shall prevail with man and with God in every area of my life, in the name of Jesus.

Every habitation of infirmity in my life, break to pieces, in the name of Jesus.

My body, soul and spirit, reject every evil load, in Jesus' name.

Evil foundation in my life, I pull you down today, in the mighty name of Jesus.

Every inherited sickness in my life, depart from me now, in the name of Jesus.

Chapter 2 - How to Live by the Grace of God

Every evil water in my body, get out, in the name of Jesus.

By the blood of Jesus, I cancel the effect of every evil dedication in my life, in the name of Jesus.

Holy Ghost fire, immunize my blood against satanic poisoning, in the name of Jesus.

Father Lord, put self control in my mouth, in the name of Jesus.

I refuse to get accustomed to sickness, in the name of Jesus.

Every door open to infirmity in my life, be permanently closed today, in the name of Jesus.

Every power contenting with God in my life, be roasted, in the name of Jesus.

Every power preventing God's glory from manifesting in my life, be paralysed, in the name of Jesus.

I loose myself from the spirit of desolation, in the name of Jesus.

Father Lord break me through in my home, in the name of Jesus.

Father Lord keep in me healthy, in the name of Jesus.

Father Lord break me through in my business, in the name of Jesus.

Let God be God in my economy, in the name of Jesus.

Glory of God, envelope every department of my life, in the name of Jesus.

The Lord that answereth by fire, be my God, in the name of Jesus.

By the blood of Jesus, all my enemies shall scatter to rise no more, in the name of Jesus.

Blood of Jesus, cry against all evil gatherings arranged for my sake, in the name of Jesus.

Chapter 2 - How to Live by the Grace of God

Father Lord, convert all my past failures to unlimited victories, in the name of Jesus.

Lord Jesus, create room for my advancement in every area of my life.

All evil thoughts against me, Lord turn them to be good for me.

Father Lord, give evil men for my life where evil decisions have been taken against me, in the name of Jesus.

Father Lord, advertise Your dumbfounding prosperity in my life.

Let the showers of dumbfounding prosperity fall in every department of my life, in the name of Jesus.

By the blood of Jesus, I claim all my prosperity in the name of Jesus.

Every door of my prosperity that has been shut, be opened now, in the name of Jesus.

Father Lord, convert my poverty to prosperity, in the name of Jesus.

Father Lord, convert my mistake to perfection, in the name of Jesus.

Father Lord, convert my frustration to fulfillment, in the name of Jesus.

Father Lord, bring honey out of the rock for me, in the name of Jesus.

By the blood of Jesus, I stand against every evil covenant of sudden death, in the name of Jesus.

By the blood of Jesus, I break every conscious and unconscious evil covenant of untimely death, in the name of Jesus.

You spirit of death and hell, you have no document in my life, in the name of Jesus.

You stones of death, depart from my ways, in the name of Jesus.

Father Lord, make me a voice of deliverance and blessing.

Chapter 2 - How to Live by the Grace of God

By the blood of Jesus, I tread upon the high places of the enemies, in the name of Jesus.

I bind and render useless, every blood sucking demon, in the name of Jesus.

You evil current of death, loose your grip over my life, in the name of Jesus.

By the blood of Jesus, I frustrate the decisions of the evil openers in my family, in the name of Jesus.

Fire of protection, cover my family, in the name of Jesus.

Father Lord, make my way perfect, in the name of Jesus.

Throughout the days of my life, I shall not be put to shame, in the name of Jesus.

By the blood of Jesus, I reject every garment of shame, in the name of Jesus.

By the blood of Jesus, I reject every shoe of shame, in the name of Jesus.

By the blood of Jesus, I reject every head-gear and cap of shame, in the name of Jesus.

Shamefulness shall not be my lot, in the name of Jesus.

Every demonic limitation of my progress as a result of shame, be removed, in the name of Jesus.

Every network of shame around me, be paralysed, in the name of Jesus.

Those who seek for my shame shall die for my sake, in the name of Jesus.

As far as shame is concerned, I shall not record any point for satan, in the name of Jesus.

In the name of Jesus, I shall not eat the bread of sorrow, I shall not eat the bread of shame and I shall not eat the bread of defeat.

No evil will touch me throughout my life, in the name of Jesus.

Chapter 2 - How to Live by the Grace of God

By the blood of Jesus, In every area of my life, my enemies will not catch me, in the name of Jesus.

By the blood of Jesus, In every area of my life, I shall run and not grow weary, I shall walk and shall not faint.

Father Lord, in every area of my life, let not my life disgrace You.

By the blood of Jesus, I will not be a victim of failure and I shall not bite my finger for any reason, in the name of Jesus.

Holy Spirit of God, Help me O Lord, to meet up with God's standard for my life.

By the blood of Jesus, I refuse to be a candidate to the spirit of amputation, in the name of Jesus.

By the blood of Jesus, with each day of my life, I shall move to higher ground, in the name of Jesus.

Every spirit of shame set in motion against my life, I bind you, in the name of Jesus

Every spirit competing with my breakthroughs, be chained, in the name of Jesus.

By the blood of Jesus, I bind every spirit of slavery , in the name of Jesus.

By the blood of Jesus, In every day of my life, I disgrace all my stubborn pursuers, in the name of Jesus.

By the blood of Jesus, I bind, every spirit of Herod, in the name of Jesus.

Every spirit challenging my God, be disgraced, in Jesus' name.

Every Red Sea before me, be parted, in the name of Jesus.

By the blood of Jesus, I command every spirit of bad ending to be bound in every area of my life, in the name of Jesus.

By the blood of Jesus, Every spirit of Saul, be disgraced in my life, in the name of Jesus.

Chapter 2 - How to Live by the Grace of God

By the blood of Jesus, Every spirit of Pharaoh, be disgraced in my life, in Jesus' name.

By the blood of Jesus, I reject every evil invitation to backwardness, in Jesus' name.

By the blood of Jesus, I command every stone of hindrance in my life to be rolled away, in the name of Jesus.

Father Lord, roll away every stone of poverty from my life, in the name Jesus.

Let every stone of infertility in my marriage be rolled away, in the name of Jesus.

Let every stone of non-achievement in my life be rolled away, in the name of Jesus.

My God, roll away every stone of hardship and slavery from my life, in the name of Jesus.

My God, roll away every stone of failure planted in my life, my home and in my business, in the name of Jesus.

You stones of hindrance, planted at the edge of my breakthroughs, be rolled away, in the name of Jesus.

You stones of stagnancy, stationed at the border of my life, be rolled away, in the name of Jesus.

My God, let every stone of the 'amputator' planted at the beginning of my life, at the middle of my life and at the end of my life, be rolled away, in the name of Jesus.

Father Lord, I thank You for all the stones You have rolled away, I forbid their return, in the name of Jesus.

Let the power from above come upon me, in the name of Jesus.

Father Lord, advertise Your power in every area of my life, in the name of Jesus.

Father Lord, make me a power generator, throughout the days of my life, in the name of Jesus.

Let the power to live a holy life throughout the days of my life fall upon me, in the name of Jesus.

Chapter 2 - How to Live by the Grace of God

Let the power to live a victorious life throughout the days of my life fall upon me, in the name of Jesus.

Let the power to prosper throughout the days of my life fall upon me, in the name of Jesus.

Let the power to be in good health throughout the days of my life fall upon me, in the name of Jesus.

Let the power to disgrace my enemies throughout the days of my life fall upon me, in the name of Jesus.

Let the power of Christ rest upon me now, in the name of Jesus.

Let the power to bind and loose fall upon me now, in the name of Jesus.

Father Lord, let Your key of revival unlock every department of my life for Your revival fire, in the name of Jesus.

Every area of my life that is at the point of death, receive the touch of revival, in the name of Jesus.

Father Lord, send down Your fire and anointing into my life, in the name of Jesus.

Every uncrucified area in my life, receive the touch of fire and be crucified, in the name of Jesus.

Let the fire fall and consume all hindrances to my advancement, in the name of Jesus.

You stubborn problems in my life, receive the Holy Ghost dynamite, in the name of Jesus.

You carry-over miracle from my past, receive the touch of fire in the name of Jesus.

Holy Ghost fire, baptize me with prayer miracle, in Jesus' name.

By the blood of Jesus, Every area of my life that needs deliverance, receive the touch of fire and be delivered, in the name of Jesus.

Let my angels of blessing locate me now, in the name of Jesus.

Chapter 2 - How to Live by the Grace of God

Every satanic programme of impossibility, I cancel you now, in the name of Jesus.

Every household wickedness and its programme of impossibility, be paralysed, in the name of Jesus.

No curse will land on my head, in the name of Jesus.

Throughout the days of my life, I will not waste money on my health: the Lord shall be my healer, in the name of Jesus.

Throughout the days of my life, I will be in the right place at the right time.

Throughout the days of my life, I will not depart from the fire of God's protection, in the name of Jesus.

Throughout the days of my life, I will not be a candidate for incurable disease, in the name of Jesus.

Every weapon of captivity, be disgraced, in the name of Jesus.

Lord, before I finish this programme, I need an outstanding miracle in every area of my life.

Let every attack planned against the progress of my life be frustrated, in the name of Jesus.

I command the spirits of harassment and torment to leave me, in the name of Jesus.

Lord, begin to speak soundness into my mind and being.

I reverse every witchcraft curse issued against my progress, in the name of Jesus.

I condemn all the spirits condemning me, in the name of Jesus.

Let divine accuracy come into my life and operations, in the name of Jesus.

No evil directive will manifest in my life, in the name of Jesus.

Let the plans and purposes of heaven be fulfilled in my life, in the name of Jesus.

Chapter 2 - How to Live by the Grace of God

O Lord, bring to me friends that reverence Your name and keep all others away.

Let divine strength come into my life, in the name of Jesus.

Let every stronghold working against my peace be destroyed, in the name of Jesus.

Let the power to destroy every decree of darkness operating in my life fall upon me now, in the name of Jesus.

Lord, deliver my tongue from evil silence.

Lord, let my tongue tell others of Your life.

Lord, loose my tongue and use it for Your glory.

Lord, let my tongue bring straying sheep back to the fold.

Lord, let my tongue strengthen those who are discouraged.

Lord, let my tongue guide the sad and the lonely.

Lord, baptise my tongue with love and fire.

Let every unrepentant and stubborn pursuers be disgraced in my life, in the name of Jesus.

Let every iron-like curse working against my life be broken by the blood of Jesus, in the name of Jesus.

Let every problem designed to disgrace me receive open shame, in the name of Jesus.

Let every problem anchor in my life be uprooted, in Jesus' name.

Multiple evil covenants, be broken by the blood of Jesus, in the name of Jesus.

Multiple curses, be broken by the blood of Jesus, in Jesus' name.

Everything done against me with evil padlocks, be nullified by the blood of Jesus, in the name of Jesus.

Chapter 2 - How to Live by the Grace of God

Everything done against me at any cross-roads, be nullified by the blood of Jesus, in the name of Jesus.

Let every stubborn and prayer resisting demon receive stones of fire and thunder, in the name of Jesus.

Every stubborn and prayer resisting sickness, loose your evil hold upon my life, in the name of Jesus.

Every problem associated with the dead, be smashed by the blood of Jesus, in the name of Jesus.

I recover my stolen property seven fold, in the name of Jesus.

Let every evil memory about me be erased by the blood of Jesus, in the name of Jesus.

By the blood of Jesus, I disallow my breakthroughs from being caged, in Jesus' name.

Let the sun of my prosperity arise and scatter every cloud of poverty, in the name of Jesus.

I decree unstoppable advancement upon my life, in Jesus' name.

I soak every day of my life in the blood of Jesus and in signs and wonders, in the name of Jesus.

I break every stronghold of oppression in my life, in Jesus' name.

Let every satanic joy about my life be terminated, in the name of Jesus.

I paralyse every household wickedness, in the name of Jesus.

Let every satanic spreading river dry up by the blood of Jesus, in the name of Jesus.

I bind every ancestral spirit and command them to loose their hold over my life, in the name of Jesus

Chapter 2 - How to Live by the Grace of God

CONCLUSION

"But when it pleased God, who separated me from my mother's womb, and called me by his grace" **Galatians1:15**

"Let no corrupt communication proceed out of your mouth, but that which is good to the use of edifying, that it may minister grace unto the hearers." **Ephesians4:29**

Unless otherwise stated, we must all come unto repentance if we must encounter our savior Jesus Christ. Repentance is the key to deliverance, protection, and promotion. Everyone that desired to encounter testimonies in their prayer must confess and forsake their sinful ways and go after God.

"Let us hear the conclusion of the whole matter: Fear God, and keep his commandments: for this is the whole duty of man. For God shall bring every work into judgment, with every secret thing, whether it be good, or whether it be evil." **Eccl12:13-14**

The entire book will remain a story to everyone who is not ready to make a decision for Jesus Christ. One man said if you failed to plan we have planned to fail in life. We want you to make plans to make heaven.

The bible says in **eccl: 12:14,** *"For God shall bring every work into judgment, with every secret thing, whether it be good, or whether it be evil."*

If you are a born again Christian; we like to encourage you in your Christian life. If you are not a born again Christian we can help you here receive genuine salvation.

"Therefore if any man be in Christ, he is a new creature: old things are passed away; behold, all things are become new." **2cor5:17**

Now repeat this prayer after me;

Say Lord Jesus, I accept you today, as my Lord and my savior, forgive me of my sins wash me with your blood. Right now, I believe, I am sanctified, I am save, I am free, I am free from the Power of sin to serve the Lord Jesus. Thank you Lord for saving me. Amen.

Chapter 2 - How to Live by the Grace of God

AGAIN I SAY TO YOU CONGRATULATIONS

What must I do to determine my divine visitation?

To determine divine visitation you must be born again. The word says as many as received him, to them gave He power to become the sons of God. Even to them that believe on his name.

To qualify for divine visitation do the following sincerely,

1) Acknowledge that you are a sinner and that He died for you. **Rom3:23**.

2) Repent of your sins. **Acts 3:19, Luke13:5, 2Peter3:9**

3) Believe in your heart that Jesus died for your sin. **Romans10:10**

4) Confess Jesus as the Lord over your life. **Romans10:10, Acts2:2**

Now repeat this Prayer after me

Say Lord Jesus, I accept you today, as my Lord and my savior, forgive me of my sins wash me with your blood. Right now, I believe, I am sanctified, I am save, I am free, I am free from the Power of sin to serve the Lord Jesus. Thank you Lord for saving me. Amen.

Congratulations: YOU ARE NOW A BORN AGAIN CHRISTIAN

AGAIN I SAY TO YOU CONGRATULATIONS

I adjure you to watch the Spirit of God bear witness with your Spirit confirming His word with signs following. The word says The Spirit itself beareth witness with our spirit, that we are the children of God.

Join a bible believing church or join us on our weekly and Sunday worship services at 343 Sanford Avenue Newark New Jersey 07106.

Chapter 2 - How to Live by the Grace of God

WISDOM KEYS

Every Productive Society is a society heading to the top

Millions of Nigerians run away from Nigeria, very few Nigerians stay in Nigeria.

My decision to return Nigeria is the will of God for my life

My short coming in America after 18 years, trained me to be wise, to think, reflect and reason appropriately.

If you train your mind to reason it will train your hands to earn money.

It is absurd to use the money of the heathen to build the kingdom of the living God.

Every Ministry reveals its agenda and goal either at the beginning or at the end. Be careful of your life it is your first Ministry.

The average American mind is conditioned for a continual quest to get new things and (discard the former) and throw away old things.

When I considered well, my BMW jeep became my initial deposit for the work of the ministry in Nigeria

Everyone is waiting for you to change your mind until you change your thinking nothing changes around you.

Multiple academic degrees in other discipline gave me the chance to think, reflect and reason

What so everyone are thinking and reflecting at the moment reveals you to the time and the now factor

All events and intents are the product of precise thought processes, accurate reason every event is designed for a designated timeline

Wisdom is your ability to think, to create and invent. If you can think wise enough you will come out of penury

The distance between you and success is your creative ability to think reason and reflect accurate.

Chapter 2 - How to Live by the Grace of God

Success is the result of hard work, commitment resolve and determination learning from past mistakes and failing.

If you organize your mind you have organized your life and destiny.

There is a thin line between success and failure. If you look above and beyond you are on your way to success.

Wealth is your ability to think, power is your ability to reason and success is your ability to be informed.

If you can make use of your mind by thinking and reasoning God will make use of your life and destiny.

Think and Be Great

Reflect, Reason, think and be great

Famous people are born of woman

That you will make it is your intention; that you will survive is your resolve, that you will succeed with changes is your determination, personal efforts and hard work.

No man was born a failure. Lack of vision is the end product of failure.

Working with mental patients encourages and aspire me to be a productive observant and dedicated to my assignment.

Successful people are not magicians, it is the will power combined with hard work, and determination and a resolve to succeed that make them succeed.

In the unequivocal state of the mind, intention is not a location or a position it is the state of the mind.

So many people think that they think. The mind is used to think reflect and reason. You will remain blind with your eye open until you can see with your mind by thinking.

There is no favoritism in accurate and precise calculation

Chapter 2 - How to Live by the Grace of God

Although knowledge is power, information is the key and gateway to a great future.

It will take the hand of God to move the hand of man.

With the backing of the great wise God, nothing will disconnect you from your inheritance.

As long as you have wisdom and understanding of God, Satan and evil cannot manipulate your life and destiny.

You have come this far by yourself judgment and decision you have made in the past, now lean and listen to God for another dimension of greatness.

Great people are common people it is extra ordinary effort and the price of sacrifice that produces greatness.

As a mental direct care worker I saw a great pastor and a motivational speaker within myself.

Menial job does not reduce your self-worth, until you resolve to achieve greatness see greatness in all you do; you will never count in your community

The principle of Jesus will solve your gambling and addiction problems

The man of Jesus will lead you into heaven,

Everyone have their self-appraisal and what they think about you. Until you discover yourself other opinion about you will alter the real you.

Supervisors and directors are just a position in the chain of command in a work place. Never allow your supervisor hierarchy to alter your opinion about yourself.

Everyone can come out of debt if they make up their mind.

That I am not a decision maker at work does not diminish my contribution to my world.

Although it appears like it was a poor decision to accept a direct care employment at a psychiatric hospital as I reflect of my nine years of experience, it became apparent that I have learnt and experienced enough for my next assignment.

Self-encouragement and determination is a resolve of the heart.

Chapter 2 - How to Live by the Grace of God

If you are determined to make a difference, and do the things that make a difference you will eventually make a difference.

Good things do not come easy

Short cuts will cut your life short.

Those who look ahead move ahead.

Life is all about making an impact. In your life time strive to make an impact in your community.

Make friends and connect with people who are moving ahead of you in life.

If you can look around well you have come a long way in your life, made a lot of difference and realized a lot of success in life.

If you are my old friend, hurry up to reach out to me before I become a stranger to you.

Everything I am blessed with inspirations from God, that change my definition and interpretation of the world around me.

I thought I was stagnant and lonely until I looked around and noticed my children running around and my wife cooking.

At 40 I resigned my Job to seek the Lord forever.

My ministry took a drastic rise to the top when the wisdom of God visited me with knowledge and understanding.

You will be a better person if you understand the characteristics of your personality – your mood swings attitudes and habits.

It is the seed of love you sow into the heart of a child and a woman that you reap in due time.

Love is not selfish, love share everything including the concealed secrets of the mind.

As long as you have a prayer life and a bible; you will never feel lonely, rejected and idle in the race of life.

When good friends disconnect from you, let them go, they might have seen something new in a different direction.

Confidence in yourself and in God is the only way to bring you out of captivity

Never train a child to waste his/her time.

The mind is the greatest assets of a great future.

Chapter 2 - How to Live by the Grace of God

You walk by common sense run by principles and fly by instruction.

Those who fly in flight of life fly alone.

Up in the air you are alone. No one can toll you accept the compass of knowledge and information

I have seen a tolling vehicle I have seen a tolling ship I have never seen a tolling airplane.

I exercise my judgment and make a decision every minute of the day.

Decisions are crucial, critical and vital with reference to your future.

So many people wish for a great future. You can only work towards a great future.

Your celebrity status began when you discovered your talent. What are you good at? Work at it with all commitment.

Prayers will sustain you but the wisdom of God will prosper you.

When I met Oyedepo, his teachings changed my perspective, but when I met Ibiyeomie; His teaching changed my perception.

I will be successful in ministry if only I concentrate and focus my energy in the work of the ministry.

It took the late Dr. Vincent Pearle Norman's book to open my mind towards kingdom success.

CHAPTER 3
PRAYER OF SALVATION

"Neither is there salvation in any other: for there is none other name under heaven given among men, whereby we must be saved." **Acts4:12.**

What must I do to determine my salvation?

To be saved we must be born again! The word says as many as received him, to them gave He power to become the sons of God. Even to them that believe on his name.

To qualify for divine visitation do the following sincerely,

1) Acknowledge that you are a sinner and that He died for you. **Rom3:23.**

2) Repent of your sins. **Acts 3:19, Luke13:5, 2Peter3:9**

3) Believe in your heart that Jesus died for your sin. **Romans10:10**

4) Confess Jesus as the Lord over your life. **Romans10:10, Acts2:21**

Now repeat this Prayer after me

Say Lord Jesus, I accept you today, as my Lord and my savior, forgive me of my sins wash me with your blood. Right now, I believe, I am sanctified, I am safe, I am free, I am free from the Power of sin to serve the Lord Jesus. Thank you Lord for saving me. Amen.

Congratulations:

YOU ARE NOW A BORN AGAIN CHRISTAIN

AGAIN I SAY TO YOU CONGRATULATION

I adjure you to watch the Spirit of God bear witness with your Spirit confirming His word with signs following. The word says The Spirit itself beareth witness with our spirit, that we are the children of God.

Chapter 3 - Prayer of Salvation

MIRACLE CARE OUTREACH

"…But that the members should have the same care one for another" **1cor12:25**

We are all members of the body of Christ. Jesus commanded us to love our neighbor as ourselves. This includes caring for one another as a member of one body. True love is expressed in caring and giving. The word says for God so Love He gave….

Reach out to someone in need of Jesus, help someone in crisis find Christ. Look out and prove your love to Jesus by caring and inviting your friends and associates to find Jesus the Healer.

Invite your friends to our Home Care Cell Fellowship (Miracle chapel Intl Satellite fellowship) In the USA at 33 Schley Street Newark New Jersey 0711

If you are in Nigeria—**MIRACLE OF GOD MINISTRIES**

**A.K.A "MIRACLE CHAPEL INTL"
Mpama –Egbu-Owerri Imo state Nigeria.**

(Home Care Cell fellowship Group). We meet every Tuesday at 6:00pm-7:00pm.

LIFE IS NOT ALL ABOUT DURATION BUT ITS ALL ABOUT DONATION

What does the above statement mean?....

"Life consists not in accumulation of material wealth.." **Luke 12:15.**

"But it's all about liberality....meaning-what you can give and share with others." **Proverb 11:25.**

When you live for others--You live forever- because you out live your generation by the legacy you live behind after you depart into glory to be with the Lord.

Chapter 3 - Prayer of Salvation

But when you live to yourself - you are reduced to self—you are easily forgotten when you die and depart in glory.

Permit me to admonish you today to live your life to be a blessing to a soul connected to you today. I want you to know that so many souls are connected and looking up to you, and through you so many souls will be saved and rescued from destruction. Will you disciple someone today to find Jesus Christ?

"As a genuine Christian; it is your duty to evangelize Jesus Christ to all you meet on your way. Jesus is still in the healing business-Jesus is still doing miracles from time of old to now.

Therefore tell someone about Jesus Christ today, disciple and bring them to Church." **John 1:45 Philip findeth Nathanael....**

Please to prove the sincerity of your love for God today; please become a soul winner. The dignity of your Christianity is hidden in your boldness to proclaim and evangelize Jesus Christ to all you meet on your way.

There is a question mark on the integrity of your Christianity until you become a life soul winner. Invite someone to join us worship the Lord Jesus this coming Sunday.

Amen

Chapter 3 - Prayer of Salvation

MIRACLE OF GOD MINISTRIES

PILLARS OF THE COMMISSION

We Believe Preach and Practice the following,

1) We believe and preach Salvation to every living human being

2) We believe and preach Repentance and forgiveness of sins

3) We believe and preach the baptism of the Holy Spirit and Spiritual gifts

4) We believe and teach the Prosperity

5) We believe and preach Divine Healing and Miracles (Signs &Wonder)

6) We believe and preach Faith

7) We believe and Proclaim the Power of God (Supernatural)

8) We believe and Proclaim Praise& Worship to God

9) We believe and preach Wisdom

10) We believe and preach Holiness (Consecration)

11) We believe and preach Vision

12) We believe and teach the Word of God

13) We believe and teach Success

14) We believe and practice Prayer

15) We believe and teach Deliverance

This 15 stones form the Pillars of Our Commission.

Become part of this church family and follow this great move of God.

MY HEART FELT PRAYER FOR YOU

It is my prayer that you testify today about the goodness of the Lord. I desire for you to have an encounter with our Lord Jesus Christ.

Chapter 3 - Prayer of Salvation

Now let me Pray for you:

Lord Jesus give this precious one reading this material heavenly vision that will give them purpose to live the remaining days of their lives. Lord God of heaven open a new chapter in the life of this precious love one reading this book today. May all their prayers be answered in the mighty name of Jesus. We thank you Jesus for hearing us. In Jesus mighty name. Amen.

WHAT TO DO WHEN MIRACLE SEEMS TO BE DELAYED:

1. Praise God even in times of trouble, trial, and tribulations.

2. Be expectant- expect God to move beyond imagination.

3) Be willing and Obedient-God look at your obedient in times of delay.

4) Be focus—God expect us to pay relevant attention to details.

5) Do not quit- If we must emerge winners, quitting is not an option.

6) Be positive—it can only get better so be positive.

7) Be optimistic--- Your case is different so be optimistic in life.

8) Develop all possibility mentality—Every limitation is within you faith.

Chapter 3 - Prayer of Salvation

TIME TO TURN TO GOD

HAVE YOU EVER ASK WHY ARE YOU HERE? GOD PLANTED YOU HERE TO BRING TO PASS HIS PLAN COUNSEL AND PLAN OVER YOUR LIFE

THE BEST OF YOUR PHYSICAL STRENGTH AND EFFORTS IS THE BEGINNING OF GODS GRACE.

ETERNITY IS REAL, HEAVEN IS SURE. BECOME INTERESTED IN HEAVENLY RACE AND BOOK YOUR NAME IN THE LAMB BOOK OF LIFE

EVERYTHING GREAT COMES BY HIS GRACE UPON YOUR LIFE.

THEREFORE TURN UNTO GOD IN SUPLICATION, IN THANKSGIVING AND IN PRAYER, AND GOD WILL TURN IN YOUR FAVOR.

CHAPTER 4
ABOUT THE AUTHOR

Rev Franklin N Abazie is the founding and Presiding Pastor of Miracle of God Ministries with headquarters in Newark, New Jersey USA and a branch church in Owerri- Imo State Nigeria. He is following the footsteps of one of his mentors, Oral Roberts (Healing Evangelist) of the blessed memory.

The Lord passed Oral Roberts healing mantle two days before he went to be with the Lord at age 91 into the hand of healing evangelist-Rev Franklin N Abazie in a vision.

In all his services the Power and Presence of God is present to heal all in his audience. He is an ordained man of God with a Healing Ministry reviving the healing and miracle ministry of Jesus Christ of Nazareth.

Chapter 4 - About the Author

Pastor Franklin N Abazie, is called by God with a unique mandate:

"THE MOMENT IS DUE TO IMPACT YOUR WORLD THROUGH THE REVIVAL OF THE HEALING & MIRACLE MINISTRY OF JESUS CHRIST OF NAZARETH.

I AM SENDING YOU TO RESTORE HEALTH UNTO THEE AND I WILL HEAL THEE OF THY WOUNDS. SAID THE LORD OF HOST"

He is a gifted ardent Teacher of the word of God who operates also in the office of a Prophet, generating and attracting undeniable signs & wonders, special miracles and healings, with apostolic fireworks of the Holy Ghost.

He is the founding and presiding senior Pastor of this fast growing Healing ministry.

He has written over 86 inspirational, healing and transforming books covering almost all aspect of divine healing and life. He is happily married and blessed with children.

BOOKS BY REV FRANKLIN N ABAZIE

1) Commanding Abundance
2) The outcome of faith
3) Understanding the secret of prevailing prayers
4) Understanding the secret of the man God uses
5) Activating my due Season
6) Overcoming Divine Verdicts
7) The Outcome of Divine Wisdom
8) Understanding God's Restoration Mandate
9) Walking in the Victory and Authority of the truth
10) Gods Covenant Exemption
11) Destiny Restoration Pillars
12) Provoking Acceptable Praise
13) Understanding Divine Judgment
14) Activating Angelic Re-enforcement
15) Provoking Un-Merited Favor
16) The Benefits of the Speaking faith
17) Understanding Divine Arrangement

18) Understanding Divine Healing
19) The Mystery of Endurance
20) Obeying Divine Instructions
21) Understanding the Voice of God
22) Never give up on Hope
23) The prevailing Power of faith
24) Understanding Divine Prosperity
25) The Reward of Prayer
26) Covenant Keys to Answered Prayers
27) Activating the Forces of Vengeance
28) Put your faith to work
29) Where is your trust?
30) The Audacity of the Blood of Jesus
31) Redeeming Your Days
32) The force of Vision
33) Breaking the shackles of Family Curses
34) Wisdom for Marriage Stability
35) The winners Faith
36) The Prayer solution
37) The power of Prayer
38) The Effective Strategy of Prayer
39) The prayer that works
40) Walking in Forgiveness
41) The power of the grace of God

42) The power of Persistence
43) Overcoming Divine verdicts
44) The audacity of the blood of Jesus.
45) The prevailing power of the blood of Jesus
46) The benefit of the speaking faith.
47) Fearless faith
48) Redeeming Your Days.
49) The Supernatural Power of Prophecy
50) The companionship of the Holy Spirit
51) Understanding Divine Judgement
52) Understanding Divine Prosperity
53) Dominating Controlling Forces
54) The winners Faith
55) Destiny Restoration Pillars
56) Developing Spiritual Muscles
57) Inexplicable faith
58) The lifestyle of Prayer
59) Developing a positive attitude in life.
60) The mystery of Divine supply
61) Encounter with God's Power
62) Walking in love
63) Praying in the Spirit
64) How to provoke your testimony

65) Walking in the reality of the Anointing
66) The reality of new birth
67) The price of freedom
68) The Supernatural power of faith
69) The Power of Persistence
70) The intellectual components of Redemption
71) Overcoming Fear
72) The Force of Vision
73) Overcoming Prevailing Challenges
74) The Power of the Grace of God
75) My life & Ministry
76) The Mystery of Praise

MIRACLE OF GOD MINISTRIES

NIGERIA CRUSADE 2012

MIRACLE OF GOD MINISTRIES

NIGERIA CRUSADE 2012

MIRACLE OF GOD MINISTRIES

NIGERIA CRUSADE

2012

MIRACLE OF GOD MINISTRIES

NIGERIA CRUSADE

2012

www.ingramcontent.com/pod-product-compliance
Lightning Source LLC
Chambersburg PA
CBHW021444080526
44588CB00009B/676